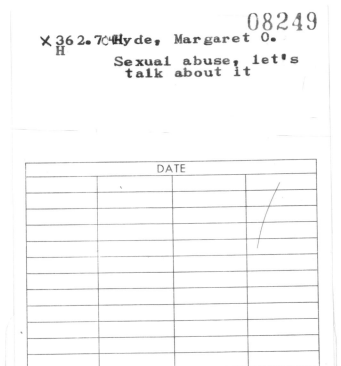

DATE			

Sexual
Abuse
LET'S TALK ABOUT IT

Westminster Press Books by
Margaret O. Hyde

Sexual Abuse—
Let's Talk About It

Is This Kid "Crazy"?
Understanding Unusual Behavior

Cry Softly!
The Story of Child Abuse

With Lawrence E. Hyde

Cancer in the Young:
A Sense of Hope

MARGARET O. HYDE

Sexual Abuse

LET'S TALK ABOUT IT

THE WESTMINSTER PRESS
Philadelphia

Book Design by Anthony Frizano

Published by The Westminster Press®
Philadelphia, Pennsylvania

PRINTED IN THE UNITED STATES OF AMERICA
9 8 7 6 5

Library of Congress Cataloging in Publication Data

Hyde, Margaret Oldroyd, 1917–
    Sexual abuse—let's talk about it.

    Bibliography: p.
    Includes index.
    SUMMARY: Discusses the sexual abuse of children, how they can protect themselves, where they can seek help, the kinds of help available, and how to increase public awareness of this program.
    1. Child molesting—United States—Juvenile literature. 2. Child molesting—United States—Prevention—Juvenile literature. 3. Child abuse—Services—United States—Juvenile literature. [1. Child molesting. 2. Child abuse] I. Title.
HQ72.U53H93 1984   362.7'044   83-27346
ISBN 0-664-32713-3

To Connie Carpenter
who is always grateful
for the opportunity of assisting young women
with special needs

CONTENTS

F O R E W O R D

Sexual abuse of children is emerging as one of the major kinds of child abuse. Since many people have found the subject too dreadful to talk about, it was easy for them to think that it rarely happened. New research indicates that one girl in four and one boy in six will be sexually abused before the age of eighteen. Victims range in age from infancy to adolescence.

Discussion about sexual abuse is no longer taboo. With new awareness of the true dimensions of the problem, this subject is beginning to receive the attention necessary for real progress toward prevention and treatment.

Even young children can be taught to protect themselves from sexual assault. They can be enlightened without being frightened. Parents who teach their children how to avoid traffic accidents, poisons, and fires are finding new programs that help them teach about good and bad touching. They emphasize the rights of children to say no to adults who make sexual advances and they encourage children to confide in a trusted person as quickly as possible.

As part of a sensitive discussion of the problem of sexual abuse, this book provides information on protection, prevention, and treatment through many case studies. It shows how children and young adults can lead the attack against sexual abuse by learning how to protect themselves, where to go for help, what kinds of help are available, and how to increase public awareness of the problem in their communities.

Knowing about sexual abuse of children can help to remove the secrecy that protects the offender and can help to prevent lasting emotional damage to the victims.

ELIZABETH HELD FORSYTH, M.D.
Child Psychiatrist

WHAT IS
SEXUAL ABUSE?

More than one child in ten in the United States is sexually abused before the age of eighteen. It may be that one in four is more accurate, but how can a person be accurate in talking about the best-kept secret in the world? Much of this tragedy need not be. There are ways in which children can protect themselves. Knowing about sexual abuse is the first step.

Will talking about such a subject be frightening? Since most abuse begins before children are twelve years old, education must begin early. Experiments have shown that children can learn to deal with the problem of sexual abuse much as they learn how to avoid traffic on a busy street, learn to respect fire, and accept other safety precautions.

Sexual abuse of children has been the best-kept secret in the world, because most people found it too difficult to consider that such a problem existed. Today, many persons are willing to recognize that there is, and has been, an epidemic of sexual abuse of children. Many children who were silent for years are speaking out in answer to surveys that reach them as adults. Some children are learning to tell about experiences soon after they occur. These new attitudes provide hope that there may come a day when offenders will no longer be able to use secrecy as protection.

For years, society turned away from a larger problem that was too horrible to believe. Even doctors accepted bizarre tales from parents who blamed long-bone fractures, unusual-looking bruises, and odd burn marks on their children on unusual accidents, such as falls from ladders, falls from bicycles, and scalds from hot water. Many of these stories did not fit the injuries, and some doctors began to suspect that some broken bones and bruises were not so accidental. After several doctors reported their suspicions, and after Dr. C. Henry Kempe introduced the idea of the battered child syndrome in 1962, the problem of child abuse became the concern of many. Doctors, nurses, teachers, social workers, community volunteers, and others contributed time and money to a movement for prevention and the treatment of victims. But, for many of these people, sexual abuse was even more difficult to confront than physical violence. This is true even though some researchers suspect that it is more common.

Many parents believe that their children will never be sexually abused because they rarely hear about incidents. It *is* true that most children will never be sexually abused, even though the amount of abuse is so widespread that it is often described as staggering. If the same number of children were suffering from a disease, alarms would be sounded against the epidemic. But the sexually abused boys and girls, who range in age from infancy to adolescence, remain largely hidden.

Relatively few parents know that prevention involves more than warnings about strangers who lure little children into such situations with offers of rides and candy. It is a myth that most cases of sexual abuse involve strangers. However, in recent years, an increasing number of parents have been instructing their children in ways that help them to avoid becoming victims of sexual abuse.

Consider the case of Linda, a child whose parents were aware of the extent of the sexual abuse problem. Six-year-old Linda stopped at Bob's house on her way home from school to show him the picture she had drawn of her favorite friend, Tim. She often stopped to see Bob, who lived just a block away and often baby-sat for her. Since Bob worked at night, he could take care of her until her mother got home from work. Bob had finished college last year, and he was proud of his first job at the computer company. Linda liked the games he let her play on his computer.

When Linda showed Bob the picture of Tim, he praised her for her good work. He suggested that they play a new computer game while Linda drank her milk and ate her cookies. This game would be special. It would be a secret between the two of them. When the game began, Bob drew a picture of Tim on the computer screen that looked very much like the one Linda had made in school. Then he added a few lines. He said that these would show that Tim was a boy. Next he pointed to his lap and said he was going to show Linda exactly what boys looked like. Bob had a strange look on his face when he said this, and Linda became very uncomfortable. She felt so frightened that she ran home without finishing her milk and cookies.

Linda told her mother what had happened at Bob's house as soon as she reached home. Her mother told her that she had done the right thing. Bob was wrong in trying to play that kind of game with her, and she would never have Bob as a sitter again. Linda was not sure why she felt so uncomfortable, but her mother explained that Bob had no right to try to involve her in sexual activity.

The kind of game Bob tried to play with Linda was a form of abuse that many children experience. Unfortunately, there are mothers who do not believe their children when they tell them about this kind of experience. This is especially true if the offender is a friend of the family. When more parents realize that they are not alone in such situations, they are more likely to take action to help their children.

Sexual abuse takes many forms, but much of it can be prevented if children and young adults learn about this kind of abuse before it happens to them. Even two-year-olds can have some understanding of how to avoid inappropriate touching. Unfortunately, most children only learn about it after it happens to them, for almost everyone finds it difficult to believe that an adolescent or adult would involve a child in any kind of sexual activity. One reason that individuals deny the existence of sexual abuse is their difficulty in dealing with the problem. Even when it happens to someone they know, many adults still find it impossible to believe that the situation happened. This is one reason why it is hard to obtain a true picture of the problem.

Although statistics about a subject that remains largely secret can be expected to differ, reporting has increased several hundredfold in recent years. Now that some of the voices of victims are beginning to be heard, many definitions of sexual abuse are being discussed.

Perhaps sexual abuse is defined in many ways because there are many kinds of such abuse. One common definition states that sexual abuse is any inappropriate suggestion or actual sexual exposing or touching between adult and child. Another definition states that it is forcing, manipulating, or tricking someone into sexual contact. The broader and preferred definition of the National Center on Child Abuse and Neglect reads: "Sexual abuse consists of contacts or interactions between a child and an adult when the child is being used for the sexual stimulation of that adult or of another person."

Sexual abuse may be committed by a person under the age of eighteen when that person is either older than the victim or when the abuser is in a position of power or control over another child.

The contact in sexual abuse may involve touching or it may be a nontouching offense. Gertrude's case is an example. Gertrude noticed that her uncle would stand near the doorway of her bedroom when she was undressing so that he could watch her. She soon learned to close the door. One evening when this uncle was visiting, he offered to bring some soda and potato chips to her room for a nighttime snack while she was getting ready for bed. Gertrude said no thank you, politely but firmly. After that, whenever her uncle was in the house, she was careful never to run down the hall to the bathroom unless she was completely dressed.

Spying on a child and suggesting that a child undress in front of an adult are two kinds of non-touching sexual offenses. When adults expose themselves in front of children in a manner known as exhibitionism, or when they make obscene phone calls or communicate with children in some other way for immoral purposes, they are sexually abusing them. These kinds of abuse are less obvious than the touching kind, but they, too, can hurt a child and leave long-lasting scars.

If adults can learn to believe in the reality of sexual abuse, much emotional pain can be prevented. Dr. Roland Summit, an outstanding psychiatrist who works in the field of sexual abuse, believes that unless adults become more aware and take action to prevent such abuse, children will continue to suffer in helpless silence. In the past, teachers, doctors, mental health workers, police, judges, and others in the adult world who dealt with reported abuses frequently found some reason to defend the adult against the child. Although many adults continue to believe that there is no such "monster in the closet," that monster is gradually being exposed by the increasing number of people who are willing to admit that it does exist.

People of all ages can contribute toward real progress in the prevention and treatment of this serious form of child abuse. You can help to prevent the vicious cycle, for some children who have been sexually abused grow up to pass on this kind of behavior to their own or other children. Dispelling the myths about sexual abuse is a beginning.

Do You Believe These Statements?

Sex offenders are usually dirty old men. (Page 34)

Sex offenders are weird-looking. (Page 36)

Most sex offenders are dependent on alcohol and/or other drugs. (Page 35)

Most child molesters are homosexuals. (Page 34)

Victims of sex crimes somehow "asked for it." (Pages 28–29)

Most victims of child sexual abuse are attractive little girls. (Page 29)

Sex offenders are usually lonely, unmarried men. (Page 36)

17

The sexual abuse of children is something new. (Page 12)

Victims of sexual abuse are weak girls who like it. (Pages 33, 54)

Most sexual assault of children is committed by strangers. (Page 35)

Sexual abuse is committed mainly for sexual pleasure. (Page 24)

Information about sexual abuse of children increases their chances of being abused. (Page 61)

Sexual abuse happens mostly at night. (Page 21)

If victims of child sexual abuse talk about it, it will make things worse. (Page 28)

Victims of sex crimes are "ruined." (Page 53)

You will find the answers to these questions in these pages. We have added page numbers to help you.

TOUCHING CAN
BE FUN

Touching can be a happy way of expressing good feelings. Touching that means caring or comfort is both nice and needed. Mothers cuddle their babies in their arms as soon as they are born, with a kind of touching that plays an important part in their future lives. Babies who are born prematurely are touched by parents and nurses to help them grow and thrive. A list of good kinds of touches is long, for touch can help to stop pain, lift a person's spirits, help to heal, and make a person feel welcome. Shaking hands, pushing a person on a swing, holding hands, petting a dog or a cat, and kissing can be wonderful ways of touching.

Young people are very open about their feelings, and freely give love by touching and hugging. They enjoy warm hugs with their parents and grandparents that say, "You are wonderful." Sometimes ball-players hug each other to express their joy in winning a game, and a huddle in a football game is a kind of touching that helps the team. Single-arm hugs are popular with friends and sisters. Perhaps your family enjoys a sandwich hug with a small person between two large ones. You can probably add many enjoyable kinds of touches to this list.

Good touching feels warm, safe, and happy. While many adults greet their friends with warm embraces, there are some adults who find it very hard to receive such friendly greetings. They seem to shy away from a pat on the back or an arm around their shoulders that is meant to comfort. Perhaps this is partly due to the fact that their parents seldom touched them, and they do not know how to tell the difference between good touches and bad touches. Many such adults treat their children much the way their parents treated them. They do not hug their children, seldom kiss them good night, and cannot express their love for them in a physical way. They may not realize that they have a problem about touching, but they are often described as cold, as standoffish, as living in their own special worlds. Sometimes, these people have had bad experiences with touching when they were young, although certainly this is not always true.

How can you tell what is good touching and what is bad touching? Sometimes children are kissed when they do not want to be. This often happens when a strange aunt or a friend of the child's parent gushes and kisses. Unfortunately, most children have to learn to put up with this in order to be polite, but sometimes a parent understands and mentions that

20

the child does not like to be kissed, meaning, of course, with the kind of kiss from that person. Much the same is true when well-meaning people pinch little cheeks in what the adults believe to be a friendly gesture. Another kind of touch that can be annoying is tickling after a child wants the tickling to stop. Much the same is true of playful wrestling that continues after one person wants to stop.

Some children have a more serious touching problem. This happens when an adult's kisses are too lingering, too sloppy, or in the wrong places. Sometimes a man may want a child to touch his genital area (his sex organs) or try to touch a child's genital area. Even young children feel that this is scary and it makes them uncomfortable.

Six-year-old Jerry was taught to submit politely when his aunt and uncle kissed him. He was told to obey his teacher no matter what she told him. And he had no choice about playing with the daughter of his mother's best friend, even though he did not like her. From the time he was a baby, Jerry's mother proudly instilled in him the importance of doing whatever an adult said, unless that adult was a stranger. When the man at the grocery store told Jerry to go into the back room with him to help him look for the new kittens, Jerry was pleased. He was not so pleased when the man told him to drop his pants, but he was obedient. The man at the grocery store was not a stranger, but Jerry did not like the secret game that the grocer insisted that he play. Jerry did not tell anyone about the secret game, since the grocer said

21

he would deny it if he ever told. Jerry kept wishing that his mother would not send him to that store on errands.

Rick's mother taught him to obey adults, but she was careful to talk to him about the times when he should not do what an adult said. She played "What if?" games with him, so when he was in a situation like Jerry's he knew what to do. Time and time again, his mother had said that he did not have to let anyone touch his private parts. He knew that he could say, "Please do not touch me there."

All children should be aware of the fact that they have rights to the privacy of the parts of their bodies that are covered by bathing suits. They can learn the following rules at a very early age:

No one has a right to touch your body in any place that you do not want it touched. You are a separate person, and you have the right to say you do not want that kind of touch. Even a very young child can learn to say, "Please do not touch me there."

Unfortunately, many parents do not know how to talk to their children about inappropriate touching. No one ever talked to them about such things. The touching problem has been such a hush-hush problem that parents tend to avoid telling their children what to do and say when these things happen to them.

Sometimes children are forced or tricked into bad touching by adults or older boys and girls who promise them treats. A baby-sitter may offer to let a child watch television in order to get cooperation. An older boy or man may ask a child to go with him into the bushes to look for his dog. Or he may offer to show the child something in the basement of his house. A stranger may ask a child to ride along with him to find a place, after asking directions. Children who have been warned about such people know enough to refuse and report these things to parents, teachers, or others.

In 75 percent of the cases of sexual abuse, the offender is known to the child. This makes it awkward for many children to say no when asked to do something they feel is uncomfortable. In some cases, children are so hungry for attention and affection that they willingly comply with an adult's secret game of touching, even though they feel it is out of bounds.

Susie always felt that she was an ugly child. She had been sick many times when she was very young, and her illness made demands of time and money on her family. Susie felt that she was unworthy of all they did for her, and there had been one time when she overheard her mother complaining about the extra attention that she needed. Susie's mother always seemed to be in a hurry to get away from the house, and Susie felt that she was an unwanted burden. Her mother took good care of Susie's physical needs, but never expressed any love for her. On the other hand, Susie's father seemed to take a special interest in her. He liked to bathe her when she was ill, but his attentions were more than fatherly. Susie enjoyed the approval from her father in the form of sexual activity, although she felt that she was bad for indulging in their secret love games. Susie just had a special feeling that the kind of touching she received from her father was not the right kind of touching, but he had made her promise not to tell about their special relationship.

The sexual touching between Susie and her father fulfilled their needs for closeness, warmth, and nurturing love. Susie did not want anyone to find out about it, because she had heard that fathers can be put in jail for loving their daughters that way. Even if he were just asked to leave the house and go for counseling, Susie knew she would cry herself to sleep every night, because she would miss him so much. Still, Susie was not comfortable about the things that were happening. She was withdrawing from her friends, hated school and skipped it many days, and was having trouble sleeping. She knew that she felt some shame and guilt, and that her father's touching was a bad substitute for the right kind of touching.

Since children are often tricked and manipulated into bad kinds of touching, they may not be hurt physically. People may say: "If you don't do this, I won't love you"; "If you tell, I'll say it was your fault." Bribes of candy, toys, and special privileges are common. And sometimes, the child wants to cooperate just to help the person who tells a story of needing the child's cooperation. Often, children just do not want to hurt the feelings of the adult, not realizing that their own feelings may be in a state of turmoil for years to come.

24

Some recent studies indicate that more children may be physically hurt by sexual abuse than formerly supposed. According to Dr. Gene G. Abel, director of the Sexual Behavior Clinic of the New York State Psychiatric Institute at Columbia-Presbyterian Medical Center in New York City, 50 percent of all child molestation may involve violence. However, the physical violence is not the only damage done to the child. In case after case of sexual abuse, long-standing emotional problems have appeared. A study by the National Institute of Mental Health recently revealed that many individuals diagnosed as schizophrenics developed multiple personalities as a way of distancing themselves from long-term child abuse. Much trouble can be avoided if children learn that they deserve to be respected.

While children have a right to be touched in nice ways, they also have a right to stop confusing and bad kinds of touching. This is true whether the touching comes from a parent, an adult whom they respect, an older brother or sister, a stranger, or anyone.

Three

SOME KINDS OF SECRETS SHOULD BE TOLD

Joan had a special friend named Jim, who had lured her into sexual activity when she was just four years old. Thirteen-year-old Jim was a neighbor whose family was very friendly with Joan's family. Jim, who was a very shy person, seemed to enjoy playing with Joan more than with boys his own age. Jim had convinced Joan that their secret game was something that made her special to him, and she was happy to have the extra attention, even though she thought it strange that Jim was so insistent about keeping the secret. As they grew older, Joan and Jim continued to spend some time alone and Jim's advances toward Joan's person increased. Joan began to feel guilty about the pleasure this gave her. She felt that she was bad, that she should probably tell her parents, but at this point, they would put all the blame on her. Maybe they wouldn't believe her, anyway. So Joan continued to cooperate with Jim, even though she began to hate their encounters. She felt dirty, ashamed, immoral, and sometimes she thought she was crazy. Joan was certain that such things never happened to other children. This made her feel different, and it affected her schoolwork, her disposition, and her general health.

Joan's feelings were not unusual. Almost every girl who is sexually abused thinks that she is the only one to whom such a thing has happened. Almost every victim considers herself bad and loses trust in adults. Almost every girl continues to feel that something is wrong with her, even when she becomes an adult, unless she has help from someone who is trained to help in such situations.

Some children feel guilty about sexual encounters they have had with adults because their feelings may be confused. On the one hand, they object to the adult taking advantage of them, swearing them to secrecy. They feel they are doing something wrong, and they are uncomfortable with their behavior. On the other hand, because enjoyment is a natural response to sexual stimulation, they may feel very guilty about enjoying a sensation or action that they think is wrong or bad. The children may conclude that they are bad or evil, and that they are at fault. Open discussions of sexual abuse help to prevent guilt and self-blame.

Adults who were molested as children commonly speak to their therapists in the following ways: "I still feel dirty." "It was so ugly that even the memories are disgusting." "I felt helpless and frightened, but I just didn't know how to handle the situation." "It was very depressing. I never felt the same again."

Unfortunately, many victims of sexual abuse do not get help until years after their experiences, but the sooner the help is made available, the better. For this reason, parents, social workers, teachers, and others who work in the area of child abuse stress the importance of telling someone right away, even if a child is merely approached and no actual abuse occurs.

Telling someone right away can accomplish two things. It can help the child deal with feelings of repulsion, shame, anxiety, anger, fear, and guilt. And it can prevent further occurrences. However, the many children who remain silent may do so because they are obeying the command to keep the secret. Since the offender emphasizes secrecy, the child often fears loss of love or retaliation from the offender. If the offender is the father, the young child may fear isolation from the home, feel the need to protect the father or the mother, or feel certain that the mother will not believe her.

Many children do not tell because they feel so completely helpless. The child may have positive feelings for the parent but negative feelings about the sexual experience. These mixed feelings appear to play an important part in the child's silence. She is overpowered by an adult whom she trusted, and her helplessness may result in her being immobilized. She may pretend to be asleep when the father comes to her bed. Many people question why children do not cry out to the mother, who is often in the next room, but the child may feel that she is to blame in some way. She may feel that she has invited the father's or stepfather's attentions, not realizing that it is always the responsibility of the older person to refrain from even the most seductive child. But a child, finding it impossible to believe that a parent is bad, decides that she must be the bad one.

Four studies indicate that the most common ages at which a child is first approached by a family member are 8.5, 10.7, 11, or 13 years. No matter which figure is most accurate, the surveys show that a great many young children must be struggling with serious problems from sexual abuse. There are children of all ages for whom the experience is a continuing one. Imagine a third-grade girl lying awake in her bed, night after night, hoping that she will not be forced into some kind of sexual activity by a male family member. She begins to hate herself, feeling that she no longer deserves respect or caring. She feels worthless, but she does not dare cry out to protect herself.

In spite of the many unpleasant feelings experienced by sexually abused children, studies indicate that most of these children keep the "secret." Dr. Henry Giarretto, an outstanding authority in the field, made a survey of twelve hundred college-age women. Of this group, 26 percent reported a sexual experience before the age of thirteen years, and only 6 percent of these incidents had been reported to authorities. In a study involving both girls and boys,

63 percent of the girls and 73 percent of the boys did not tell anyone about their experiences.

Apparently, most children do not tell *anyone* after they have been sexually abused. The only time that many victims can bring themselves to provide information about sexual abuse is many years later, when they are asked to answer questions in surveys. Studies show that their secrets have remained hidden from parents, brothers, sisters, friends, and doctors. Although surveys can give some picture of the percentage of children involved in sexual abuse, no one can guess how many children who have suffered remain forever silent.

Since a parent, other relative, or family friend may be involved, it is not surprising that most cases of sexual abuse are never reported to the police. Public exposure could mean humiliation and perhaps the breaking up of a family, along with punishment for the offender. Very young children may not consider these possibilities, but almost all victims are afraid that they will not be believed or that they will be blamed. This is not without reason, for many parents do defend the adult offender. One father refused to have his child in the house after she had been raped, because he felt that he had been dishonored. This is typical of the men who still feel that the women and girls in their families are their property. One mother gave her child a beating because she was involved in sexual activity with an older man.

Although reactions to the child who tells about

sexual abuse often lack understanding, there is an increasing awareness among parents that sexual abuse is never the child's fault. With adults' new willingness to face the problem, the myth of placing blame on children is gradually being exposed for what it is. Only adults who fear talking about sexual abuse are likely to overlook it or deny that a problem exists when a child tries to tell them about it.

When Dr. Vincent DeFrancis reported reactions of parents in a study in 1969, the single most common response of parents concerned the offender (about 35 percent). Only 14 percent of the parents were most concerned about the child. About 19 percent of the parents were most concerned about themselves, 6 percent were indifferent, and 8 percent were immobilized. Parents whose response concerned the offender were either angry with the offender and wanted him to be punished, or they wanted to protect the offender and blamed the child for leading him on.

Results of a more recent study were reported by Professor David Finkelhor in April 1983. Five hundred twenty-one Boston families were interviewed by the Center for Survey Research, an organization sponsored jointly by Harvard University and the Massachusetts Institute of Technology. The investigators found that the parents were surprisingly well informed about the existence of child sexual abuse. About one parent in ten said that his or her own children had been victims of abuse or attempted abuse and nearly half of the parents knew a child who had been a victim. (The actual number of victims is estimated to be about twice as many, or one in five.) This reaction to the problem was quite different from that of parents in earlier studies. Most of the parents in the Boston survey rated sexual abuse as a more harmful experience than the death of a friend or divorce in the family. They overwhelmingly supported education in their children's schools about sexual abuse. About 93 percent of these parents had been exposed to discussions of the sexual victimization of children within the previous year, mainly through television programs or newspaper articles.

Although the parents were surprisingly knowledgeable about the extent of sexual abuse, and although they were greatly concerned about it, relatively few had talked with their children about the subject. Hardly any of the parents had discussed the subject with children under the age of nine, although a sizable number of children below this age are abused.

Part of the problem in helping very young children results from their inability to tell about the experience. But parents who are aware of the problem of sexual abuse can often catch the message even though it is disguised. For example, a child might say, "Uncle Greg wears funny underwear." Or, "I don't like Mr. Smith anymore." Such statements may not necessarily be a way of telling about sexual abuse, but careful questioning by a parent can reveal their true nature. The child whose parent is sensitive to such signals is far more fortunate than one whose mother responds, "I never want to hear that kind of talk again."

Again and again, parents need to emphasize that it is not the fault of the child if someone touches her or him in a way that is confusing or uncomfortable. Playing "What if" games is a good way to teach young children how to respond to lures. Children should be taught to tell parents about any attempted sexual abuse, but if parents do not listen, they can tell a school nurse, a teacher, a doctor, a religious leader. Experts in the field of sexual abuse prevention suggest that children should continue to tell until someone does listen and believes them. Such secrets should be told.

WHO WOULD DO SUCH A THING?

The thought of a child being sexually abused is so difficult to accept that the offender is almost always pictured as a monster in human form. Is he an old man in a wrinkled raincoat who gives candy to little children so he can lure them to some isolated place? Is he a homosexual who takes advantage of little boys? Is he some kind of sex fiend?

There is no simple profile of a typical sex offender. In fact, many of the common descriptions of sexual abusers have been shown to be incorrect. For example, the belief that most sex offenders fit the description of a "dirty old man" is a myth. It *is* true that most offenders are male, although experts believe that there may be more female abusers than it was formerly believed. But it is not true that offenders are mainly old men. In some studies, the median age of the males is thirty-one years. About 21 percent of recognized offenders are under the age of twenty and only 10 percent are over fifty years of age. In one report, over half the children referred to the Child Protection Center of Children's Hospital National Medical Center in Washington, D.C., were victimized by offenders under the age of eighteen.

Adolescent offenders who have been studied tend to fall into two groups. One type is undersocialized and not aggressive; the other is involved with a peer group, uses force or violence, and is often involved with alcohol and other drugs. Boys in the latter group are not apt to be interested in babysitting. Parents often ask how they can spot a possible offender among the many friendly and polite boys who are interested in helping activities with young children. The majority of such boys are a great asset to society, for they genuinely enjoy working with children. Experts suggest that a telling sign of a teenage boy who might become sexually involved with a young child is his absence of activity with boys his own age. If his interest in young children is not balanced with activities that involve boys his own age, there might be reason for concern.

Many people still think of the sex offender as a stranger who lures children from schoolyards, playgrounds, and parks. However, most abuse appears to take place in the home of the offender or the victim, and in many cases this is the same place. Unpleasant truths such as this are hard to believe.

Half of the parents who were interviewed in the Boston study still believed that the abuser is usually a stranger, even though this group was surprisingly well informed about the problem in general. Estimates of the number of offenders who are known to the children they abuse vary from 65 percent to 80 percent.

Unfortunately, one cannot tell from appearance or from personality who might be an offender. Abusers may be rich or poor, bright or dull. They may be upstanding members of the community who appear "normal" in most respects. Offenders have been found among all races and economic and social groups. They have been found among scout leaders, teachers, religious leaders, baby-sitters, neighbors who enjoy being with children, and members of a child's own family. They have been identified as lawyers, plumbers, high-ranking military officers, physicians, and men from all walks of life. Of course, few such people, including those who work with children, abuse them sexually.

Mike could have been the victim of abuse by a stranger. One day when Mike was standing alone near the fence of the schoolyard during recess, a young man stopped to talk with him. The man came several times during the next week, and Mike found that he enjoyed their talks. Mike had been feeling lonely because he had argued with his friends and had decided they didn't really care about him, anyhow. One day, the young man waited for Mike until he left school at the end of the day and walked part of the way home with him. When the man asked Mike to go into the woods to look for mushrooms, Mike remembered that his mother had told him to beware of such requests. Mike ran home and from then on was careful to avoid the man whenever he saw him near the school.

Mike's case is one that most people consider to be typical. However, since the offenders in most cases of sexual abuse are known to the children, the luring of children by strangers is not so common as the gentle persuasion by men whom children trust.

The stranger who approached Mike probably had very different reasons for doing so from a father who becomes involved with his daughter. However, it is not impossible that both of these men belong to a group known as pedophiles. Pedophiles are people who have sexual cravings for children (the word means lover of children) that appear to be lifelong, uncontrollable compulsions. Only a small minority of men who become involved in incest, or the sexual abuse of children, known or unknown to them, appear to be pedophiles. Many pedophiles are more comfortable around children than around adults. These men, who suffer from low self-esteem, may feel that adult women would not be interested in them because they are too inadequate.

Pedophiles are sexually attracted to young girls or young boys, and in some cases to children of both sexes. Many men show a preference for a certain age child, and their sexual interest seldom varies from this age group. They are sometimes called fixated offenders, for even when they grow older, their sexual interests remain fixed on children of a much younger age.

Of the pedophiles studied by Dr. Nicholas

Groth, 81 percent had themselves been sexually abused as children. He believes that these men may be reenacting their own sexual victimization hoping that they can change it into a warm and loving experience. They hope to purge the original fear in a situation by creating one of which they are in control.

Many pedophiles, who see themselves in the children they befriend, tell themselves they are doing the child a favor by providing more affection than the child would receive at home. They see this as a reason for their actions rather than the seeking of the nonthreatening affection of a child.

Some people who abuse children sexually are motivated by anger or hostility toward the child or what the child represents, and these people represent a real physical threat to the children they seek out. While there is general agreement that the vast majority of abusers are not psychotics who suffer from delusions or hallucinations, there is considerable disagreement as to whether or not they suffer from a treatable illness. David Finkelhor has suggested that most of the men who commit sexual abuse know it is wrong. Some psychiatrists believe that most child molesters belong in prison rather than in a mental hospital. But a treatment approach is being used by many therapists who feel that the offenders, as well as the child victims and other members of their families, can and should be helped.

Although relatively little is known about why children are sexually victimized by strangers, there have been many studies of families in which incest takes place. In a small fraction of cases, incest appears to be an accepted part of the culture. This is believed to happen in a few isolated, mountainous regions where the oldest daughter is expected to assume the role of the mother both in household tasks and in bed. Younger daughters may be introduced to sexual activity by the father or brothers.

Men who become involved in incest are often referred to as regressed offenders. They have no special sexual interest in children until the time of the first offense, and this is often a time of special stress. In many cases, fathers or stepfathers appear to use incest as a way to experience closeness and nurturing in human contacts. In the typical family in which incest occurs, the mother either is absent or has separated herself from the husband emotionally. A daughter, usually the oldest, takes over the role of the mother after a gradual introduction to love games with the father.

Sally's father was disappointed with his life and his relationship with his wife, and he had no close friends. He considered himself a family man and had strict rules for the behavior of his wife and children. He did not plan to seduce his daughter, but he found himself becoming closer to her night after night when she would greet him fondly after a long day at work. His wife worked in the evenings, so Sally would get the dinner, put the children to bed, and snuggle next to her father while they watched television. Sally's attentions made the weak and insecure man feel strong and loved, feelings he felt his wife denied him. After his first sexual experience with Sally, he felt guilty and frightened, but he continued to repeat his actions. He managed to persuade Sally to remain silent about their secret games until years later, when she rebelled at his refusal to let her date boys her own age.

An incestuous father may rationalize that he is preparing his daughter for future experiences with young men, while, at the same time, he shows extreme jealousy if the daughter pays attention to boys her own age. Like Sally's father, most such sexual abusers are typically very strict, may appear to be extremely religious, and are very critical of their children's seeking relationships outside the family. They have poor impulse control and few social and emotional contacts outside the family. Many have a history of child abuse by one or both of their parents.

There is disagreement about whether or not the mother in such a family is a conscious ally. If she knows about what is taking place, she may not be willing to acknowledge it openly for fear of breaking up the home and losing the financial support of her husband. On the other hand, she may feel jealousy toward the daughter.

If the girl goes to the mother for help, she may find that the mother does not believe her. The denial may be due to the fact that the mother does not really believe what is happening or that she prefers to ignore it. In either case, the daughter, who may have been pleased with the father's attentions at first, but who is suffering intensely when she asks for help, is frustrated.

There are really two victims in child sexual abuse: the child and the offender. With the new awareness of the problems of sexual abuse of children, an increasing number of both are finding help from various sources.

five

BINNY'S STORY

Considering the number of people who are victims of sexual assault, there is a very good chance that you know someone who has been a victim. If a friend should tell you about an experience, would you know how to act?

Binny (not her real name) confided about her relationship with her father to her friend Molly when the two girls were walking home from the movies. Since the theme of the movie dealt with the love of a very young girl for an older man, it seemed natural for Binny to ask Molly how she would feel about loving an older man. This conversation led to the affair that Binny had been having with her father for three years. At first, Molly was so shocked that she did not know what to say. Then she realized that the best thing she could do was just to listen.

Binny did not feel that her relationship with her father was wrong; in fact, she rather enjoyed it, since it was the only affection she had ever known. It was comforting and pleasurable, but she sometimes felt that she had no control of her own body and her emotions.

As Binny talked about her situation, Molly began to understand how she could have mixed feelings about her father. Although Binny enjoyed extra gifts from her father and she felt special because of his attention, she was furious with him for being so strict about her going out with boys. Molly let Binny talk without interruption, although there were times when Binny was silent for a while. Molly found that this silence made her nervous, so she tried repeating some of the things Binny had said in the form of questions. This seemed to help her continue.

Molly tried to understand what had happened to her friend. She hated this father who had taken advantage of his daughter, but she knew that Binny still loved him. From time to time Molly reached out and put her arm around Binny's shoulder. When Binny said that she wished someone would help her and her father, Molly suggested that she confide in the counselor at school. Unfortunately, neither girl liked the counselor. Then they both decided to talk to Molly's older sister, Emily, to see what she would suggest. Emily did volunteer work at the local hospital, and she knew some of the social workers there. She would know people who could help.

When Emily suggested that Binny talk with a social worker at the hospital, Binny was frightened. She did not want to make trouble for her father, even though she desperately wanted someone to help her.

And she was ashamed to have strangers know her secret. Emily assured her that the social worker would be kind, although the case had to be reported to the legal authorities. At this point, Binny began to panic. She wondered if she had made a mistake by confiding in Molly. The whole situation seemed hopeless. Perhaps she should run away. She told her friend Molly that she planned to take the bus to New York City and get a job there. But Molly asked her to wait until she talked this over with Emily.

Molly learned that running away is a common choice of girls who are trying to get away from sexual abuse at home. Dr. Sam Janus reports in *The Death of Innocence* that at least 75 percent of the runaways, on the national average, are escaping incestuous abuse. Seventy-two percent of young prostitutes and children involved in pornography have had some experience with incest. So, many run away from one bad situation to another. Many experts believe that chronic runaways will become prostitutes. When Binny learned this, she decided to try to persuade her father to stop treating her as a lover.

Binny's father did not agree to her request. In fact, he threatened to involve her younger sisters. He also threatened to tell her mother and insisted that such information would kill her, since she was already sick. Binny did not think her mother seemed very sick, but she needed to have an end to the relationship with her father. She made up her mind to do what she had to do, and she told Emily she would talk to the social worker at the hospital. Emily reminded

Binny that she was doing this for her family as well as for herself. Fortunately, Binny lived in a community where help was available for her, her father, and all the members of her family.

When Binny's case was reported, a number of professional people became involved. A doctor, a policewoman, a social worker, and a lawyer worked together to investigate the situation. The social worker assured Binny that she had done the right thing by asking for help so that her father would not take advantage of her. Most respectable experts believe that incest is always damaging to a child in some way. Every case is different, but long-term emotional disturbance is found in many studies of victims. At the time of sexual abuse, many children become alienated from their peers, lose their self-esteem, and have difficulty in relating to the opposite sex. They may suffer severe anxiety attacks, depression, hostility, self-blame, or self-mutilation. They may indulge in excessive use of drugs or suffer from other forms of emotional disturbance. Even though not every victim of sexual assault is seriously disturbed by the experience, it is never right to take advantage of someone who is relatively powerless for one's own satisfaction. Adults who were molested as children may appear to lead normal lives, but many suffer from the effects in hidden ways. Before they reach out for help, many have trouble in maintaining lasting relationships and in holding jobs.

As Binny became increasingly certain that she never deserved what had happened to her, she began to feel that she had done the right thing by asking for help. This feeling was especially important to her when her father was asked to move from their home until he could complete some therapy. Although he felt angry, he also felt relieved. He realized that he was in need of help, but he had been afraid to ask for it.

Binny, her mother, her brothers, and her sisters all took part in the therapy program. During a period of three years, Binny and her mother were able to regain a sense of control over their own lives. Her mother and father were able to do a better job of parenting and were able to resume a more normal relationship with each other. Both of Binny's parents had been hurt emotionally by sexual abuse when they were children. The cycle might have continued if it were not for the program that helped them change their behaviors and provided support at a time when they needed to ventilate their feelings about their failures as parents. It also helped them to express their anger about their own parents.

Binny's family participated in the Child Sexual Abuse Treatment Program in their community. This program was modeled after one that was developed in Santa Clara County, California, under the direction of Dr. Henry Giarretto. It is used as a model by the Institute of the Community as Extended Family, a national training program that is available to interested professionals and community members who are committed to the development of services for sexually abused children and their families. There are more than sixty-five centers in various parts of the United States that are based on this model.

One part of the program consists of self-help groups that work with professionals and trained volunteers. Daughters and Sons United groups are children who have been sexually abused helping other children who have been sexually abused. Such groups provide member-to-member support. Some of the children are as young as five and some are as old as eighteen. Some of the children may live at home with their parents, relatives, or friends; others may live in foster homes, group homes, and children's shelters. These boys and girls are much like all other boys and girls except that they have all experienced child sexual abuse. Together, they share similar experiences and feelings. Just realizing that they are not alone is helpful. But they also know that they will be heard, understood, and accepted. The mutual support helps them to understand themselves, one another, and their families.

Group counseling is considered the most important part of the Child Sexual Abuse Treatment Program. At the beginning of many meetings, the entire group assembles to deal with organization. Then they break into smaller groups, such as those for new members, mother/daughter, father/daughter, communication skills, self-awareness, and play therapy for ages five to eight. Each group has six to ten members who meet once a week.

Daughters and Sons United encourages the formation of new chapters but stresses that such chapters are only one part of a program needed to provide essential services to the victims of child abuse and their families. They work together with the counseling program, the parents' self-help group, and the volunteer component. Anyone who wants more information about children helping children or other aspects of this Child Sexual Abuse Treatment Program should contact Parents United, P.O. Box 952, San Jose, CA 95108-0952.

There are many approaches to helping a friend who has been sexually abused and many ways in which an abused person can reach out. The sexual abuse of children hurts everyone, not just the children to whom it happens. Abused persons like Binny need the support of other young people in dispelling myths about child sexual abuse and in promoting awareness of the problem. Everyone can play a part in prevention.

WHEN THE
SECRET IS TOLD

Four-year-old Sara was playing on the front lawn when her uncle stopped to visit. He told Sara that she had a spider on her shorts, and he began to brush it away. He continued to brush, moving his hand inside her shorts. When this happened, Sara felt uncomfortable and she ran away.

Sara was frightened even when she told her mother about the problem. When the uncle was confronted, he denied doing more than brushing a spider from Sara's shorts. Her mother believed him and told Sara not to be a crybaby.

The next time this uncle visited, he spent some time in the family room with Sara watching television. When he fondled her, Sara ran upstairs and told her mother as well as she could about what had happened. This time her mother believed her, even though Sara was too young to explain exactly what had happened. She sent the uncle away and promised Sara that she would never leave her alone with him again. But Sara still seemed upset, and her mother was concerned because her daughter did not eat or sleep well. A friend suggested that she take Sara to a clinic where there were professionals trained to help in such situations.

When Sara's mother took her to the clinic at the hospital, the social worker, whose name was Ann, made friends with the little girl. Ann invited Sara to join her in the playroom, where they spent some time doing puzzles together. Then Ann suggested that they play with the dolls. These dolls were specially made with anatomical parts to resemble a male and a female. Using the dolls, Sara was able to show the social worker where her uncle had touched her and where he had forced her to touch him. Through a series of meetings, Sara was helped to regain her calm and her self-esteem. She no longer felt frightened when she saw a man who looked like her uncle, and she could get on with the task of learning how to live.

Billy was able to relate his experience to a social worker in another way. He had been warned by the man who molested him that he would be hurt if he told their secret, but Billy felt he could speak through the mouth of the puppets that were kept in a therapist's playroom. He was able to reveal information that was considered to be the cause of his acting up in school and his withdrawal from friends.

Art therapy is one of the most effective ways of helping children who are suffering from sexual assault. A therapist may use an "artmobile" that contains paints, chalk, clay, and other materials. A child is invited to use whatever he or she wishes, or is invited to work with a trained adult on a one-to-one basis. Many times a child's feelings can be recognized by what is drawn. For example, shame often appears hidden behind clown symbols. Many children draw themselves engulfed in a pattern of jagged lines that represent their angry feelings. A child who is pressured not to talk about an incident might draw a person with eyes, ears, nose, but no mouth. One child drew a picture that represented a monster kissing a girl. Bombs and whirlwinds may be an expression of furor in the home.

Professionals are taught to guard against misinterpretation of art symbols. In one case, only painstaking care and expertise revealed an actual case of sexual abuse. The child's first drawing gave no indication of assault. However, some of her conversation and her future drawings seemed to indicate sexual abuse. It was learned that her mother and sister were involved, and they enjoyed the sexual activity even though they felt guilty about it.

Although art therapists are trained to talk to children about the drawings in such a way that they are able to express many of their hidden feelings, the art therapists are usually only a part of a team in the helping professions.

Betsy was afraid to tell anyone she knew about experiences that seemed too horrible for words. In her community, Child and Family Services supported a hotline that played taped messages for children who suffered sexual abuse. When Betsy dialed the number, she was greeted with a message like the following:

> Hello, I am a family counselor with Child and Family Services. The care team for the child and teenage victim of sex abuse is for your safety. If you think you are being sexually abused, please stay on the line until this message is completed; then wait a moment and a counselor will come on the line to help you and talk to you if you wish. You don't have to give your name at any time. Only give your name if you want this call to be reported to the Tennessee Department of Human Services. You may wish to call 546-1530 and ask to report the sex abuse problem yourself or maybe you wish to talk to a school counselor or some other adult whom you trust.
>
> Let me say a few words about sex abuse. It happens in all types of families—to boys and to girls. Sex abuse may be any kind of physical contact that makes you feel uncomfortable or uneasy. In other words, if you have a feeling that something is wrong, you may be right. You are not alone with your problem. It is not your fault. You have done nothing wrong; calling this number is a big step toward help. Sex abuse is any kind of sexual fondling or play with genitals between an adult and children, an adult and teenagers, or between a child and someone only slightly older. This contact may be made by someone in your family or by a friend. It can include exposing private parts of the body.

Sometimes it means taking pictures of nude or partly nude children or teenagers.

Sex abuse is, in most cases, a problem needing professional help. It most often occurs in the home. Most of the time the adults are known to the child or teenager, and they may be family members. Most abusers, as well as the children and the families, can be successfully helped. Help is available for both the abused and the abuser. This help includes individual talk sessions with the victim as well as talk with other kids who have been sexually abused. There may also be individual and group sessions for the abuser, and family sessions to include the abused and parents.

If you have sexually abused someone, trained counselors are standing by to help you overcome the problem. If you are being sexually abused, it's not your fault. You may feel scared now, but help is available for you. Again, you don't have to give your name unless you want us to report the sex abuse for you. Please hold the line at the end of this message and a professional counselor will talk to you and help you. We only want to help you and let you help yourself. You have done nothing wrong, and you are on your way to being helped.

The above teletape was developed as a model and was demonstrated in Knoxville, Tennessee, in connection with a twenty-four-hour counseling service conducted by the local Children's Protection Services Agency under a grant from the National Center on Child Abuse and Neglect. Even if there is no such hotline in your community, the information it contains is a model for those who need help.

There is a national hotline for children who suffer from all kinds of child abuse. To call the national hotline, dial 1-800-4-A-CHILD. There are listings in the telephone books of many cities that direct people to counseling services in their own community.

A number of resources are available to young victims and for potential abusers in large cities. For example, the San Francisco Child Abuse Council suggests the following resources: Children's Emergency Services; the Police Department; Child and Adolescent Sexual Abuse Resource Centers; San Francisco Child Abuse Council; Emergency Family Care Center; T.A.L.K. Line; Parents Anonymous; Center for Special Problems; La Casa de las Madres; Legal Services for Children. Although victims and offenders in other areas may not have access to so many different resources, this list illustrates the kinds of organizations from which one might receive help.

Anyone who carefully reads the teletape model, above, will note that it repeats the message that the abused child is not to blame. It is most important for children to know that they are victims and have never deserved what has happened to them. Such understanding is important for the children and for everyone.

Knowing that the child is never to blame is especially important for anyone who serves on a jury for a trial that involves the sexual abuse of a child. When the defendant's lawyer tries to place guilt on a child for wearing seductive clothing or for enticing the abuser in some other way, a well-informed jury can discount such attempts.

Children may be twice victimized, once by the abuser and once by the court system. In recent years there has been emphasis on helping children to feel comfortable in court. In the case of six-year-old Nancy, her lawyer took Nancy into the courtroom before the trial so that she would be familiar with the surroundings. Nancy had to undergo a competency test in the judge's chambers before the trial. The judge asked her, "If I said it is raining here in court, would that be the truth or a lie?" The lawyer asked her, "If I told the judge that you hit me, would that be the truth or a lie?" Nancy had no problem recognizing the truth.

When Nancy was asked to testify about how Uncle Charlie had played hide-and-seek with her, she was prepared for the questions. She, like other children, recalled fewer details than an adult witness, but made fewer inaccurate statements. Nancy described how Uncle Charlie had told her he loved her and put his hand under her dress. Nancy told how he promised that they could play secret games together and threatened to hurt her if she told anyone.

When one of the lawyers tried to make a point about children making up stories of sexual abuse, it was brought out that children seldom fantasize about sexual incidents. Nancy admitted to telling some lies about things she had done at home and explained that she had been punished for them. Her lawyer made it clear that she knew she must tell the truth in court. It was obvious that she was able to look right at the judge and tell what really happened.

After Nancy told what had happened to her, a medical expert was called to educate the jury about the dynamics of child sexual abuse. Many of the members of the jury had thought that all such victims were "torn up inside," but the doctor explained that bed-wetting, acting out, and other common behavior problems are more often the only signals of sexual abuse beyond what the children tell.

After the doctor told the jury about the many cases of sexual abuse that he had treated, Nancy was asked to show by playacting what had happened to her. She used what he called "natural dolls" (dolls that are anatomically correct).

Before Nancy came to court, she was told that it would be up to the judge and the jury to decide what would happen to Uncle Charlie. It would be their decision, and, if he were sent to jail, Nancy would not be at fault. Nancy was relieved to find that the court was arranging to help Uncle Charlie with his problem, and she was even more relieved to know that Uncle Charlie would no longer be chasing her in what he called their secret game.

In many cases of incest, girls have tolerated sexual abuse over a period of years because of their fears. They do not want to cause their father to lose his job and the family, in turn, to lose its source of support. Even though they may be suffering from their experiences, they have mixed feelings about their father and do not want him to go to jail. They do not want to lose the father's affection, and they know that telling will cause him to be angry. This, of course, may also be true for the father, who knows that he needs help but does not know how to obtain it.

While it is important to work toward helping the victims of sexual abuse directly, there is much work to be done toward preventing such abuse from occurring in the first place.

Seven

HELPING TO PREVENT SEXUAL ABUSE

About fifty children in the elementary school auditorium are eagerly watching a play about a sensitive subject: the prevention of sexual abuse. At the beginning, they become acquainted with people of the planet Bubblyonia, where round-faced inhabitants live encased in bubbles. Because of the bubbles, Bubblyonians cannot experience the sense of touch. One of them, Bub, decides to visit Earth, where he makes friends with two actors named Archie and Betty, as well as with the children in the audience.

Archie and Betty introduce Bub to some wonderful and comfortable earthly touches, such as a hug, a warm hand, a mother's caress. Bub likes these and decides he is ready to become an Earthling. Archie and Betty disagree and warn Bub that he needs to know more about touching. So he learns about mothers who hit their children when they misbehave, and about people who get carried away with kissing and hugging so much that they hurt children.

Bub learns that bad touches can come from people who are not strangers. Betty tells him such touches just might come from a friend or a member of the family. She suggests that Uncle Clarence might touch places that are private to Bub, and he tells them that he would say, "Please don't touch me there." If Uncle Clarence held him too tightly and would not let him get up, Bub assures Archie and Betty that he would scream until someone heard him. Then he would tell.

But Bub thinks about the problem a little more. He asks, "Whom would I tell? Whom could I trust?" These questions lead to answers that children in the audience could put to use if they encountered forced sexual touching. Bub becomes a role model for the children, who find him a humorous and sensitive teacher. At the end of the play, he involves them in discussions that can help to provide ways of coping with forced sexual touch.

The play *Bubblyonian Encounter* is the result of a joint effort of Bubblyonian Productions, the Kansas Committee for the Prevention of Child Abuse, and the Johnson County Mental Health Center. It has reached many children since it was first performed in the summer of 1980. Today, it reaches a large number of audiences through the help of a touring troupe of actors and staff members. They direct the play for professional or amateur actors in communities who ask for their help. A videotape of Bubblyonian Productions is available for classroom use, private viewings, and small audiences.

One of the authors of *Bubblyonian Encounter* is SuEllen Fried, president of the National Committee for the Prevention of Child Abuse. The other is Helen Swan of the Johnson County Mental Health Center. Along with the artistic director of the play, Gene Mackey, they point out their goals as follows: (1) helping children to understand what forced sexual touch is, (2) changing their attitude so that they know sexual abuse is not their fault, (3) showing them that they have the right to tell someone until they are believed, and (4) being positive about the right kinds of touching.

In Kansas, according to Mrs. Swan, the average victim of child sexual abuse is between eight and eleven years old. Statistics indicate that one child in six in elementary school will experience some form of sexual exploitation.

Information on a new film about Bub and other materials that can help in preventing the sexual abuse of children is available in a free catalog from the National Committee for the Prevention of Child Abuse, 332 South Michigan Avenue, Suite 1250, Chicago, IL 60604-4357.

In recent years, since it has become socially acceptable to discuss the problem of sexual abuse of children, many communities have sprung into action to help young people through awareness and education. Efforts are based on the idea that children who are educated about sexual abuse are less likely to be victims.

One of the first tasks of such programs is to dispel myths about the effect of discussing the subject of sexual abuse. In Hennepin County, Minnesota, the Attorney's Office joined with the Illusion Theatre and the Minneapolis Public Schools to develop an educational program for children. The staff of the Sexual Assault Services cited the following myths about sexual abuse education that are commonly believed.

1. It is not important for children to have information on sexual assault. (False)

    Just as it is important for children to receive information to protect themselves against fires, traffic accidents, and drowning, it is important for them to have information that protects them against sexual abuse.

2. It is damaging and/or dangerous to give children information about sexual assault. (False)

    Actually just the opposite is true. Victims may be embarrassed or afraid to report sex crimes and hesitant to seek treatment because they lack information. And if they do not know what to do when approached, they are more likely to be manipulated or forced into some type of sexual contact.

3. Children are not sexual beings. (False)

    People are sexual beings from birth to death. Denying that children are sexual beings can lead to beliefs that sexual assault does not hurt them or that they do not need such information.

4. A discussion about sexual assault will scare children. (False)

Many children say that it is frightening to them to have inaccurate or sketchy information. Fear can be balanced by positive discussions. Children who have been exposed to information about sexual assault are more likely to report any incidents.

5. A discussion about sexual assault will scare children from all touch. (False)

Children who have been exposed to discussion about touch have fewer taboos about good kinds of touching and feel more comfortable about refusing the wrong kind of touch.

Activities in the Minneapolis School Project began in kindergarten with an emphasis on kinds of touching (see Chapter 2), and they continued throughout the school system through senior high school. A popular and helpful booklet for very young children was inspired by the programs of the Illusion Theatre and the Hennepin County Prevention Project. This booklet, *Red Flag, Green Flag People,* is a variation of a coloring book with text that was written by Joy Williams and illustrated by Kecia Softing. It was published by the Rape and Abuse Crisis Center of Fargo-Moorhead in Fargo, North Dakota. The booklet shows many good kinds of touches, or green flag touches, includes ways to avoid the red flag kind, and tells young children what to do if they encounter a confusing or uncomfortable touch.

Another sensitive book for very young children is called *Something Happened to Me*. In it, the author, Phyllis Sweet, gives words to the feelings of a child who has been sexually abused and suggests how to deal with the problem. Still another book, *My Very Own Special Body Book,* by Kerry Bassett, is written for preschool through third grade.

CHILDHELP USA of Woodland Hills, California, distributes booklets that are written especially for adolescent readers. One, called *No One Knew My Secret 'til One Day,* deals with the subject of sexual abuse.

These are just some of the approaches to helping young children avoid sexual abuse through the use of printed material. Addresses and some additional suggestions can be found at the end of this book.

In addition to the Bubblyonian play, a number of efforts are being made to reach young children and their parents through drama. *Touch* is the name of a drama that was developed by the Hennepin County group. It explains sexual abuse in a balanced way that is simple and nonthreatening. Although the presentation is written for children in kindergarten and grades one through eight, it provides a special kind of learning experience for people of all ages.

Touch study cards are visual aids that can be used to stimulate discussion and increase learning after children watch the drama.

The Touching Problem is another stage production that deals with kinds of touching. It was created by the Coalition for Child Advocacy of Bellingham, Washington, to show adults how to talk to children about the subject of sexual abuse. Thousands of people have watched the presentation, which was originally produced by the Soap Box Players. A videotape based on the *The Touching Problem* is available to distant communities. This is a high-impact documentary drama that illustrates why children should be taught skills to protect themselves against sexual abuse. Recently, this group has focused on presenting a special one-hour program for children in elementary schools.

No More Secrets is a film on sexual abuse for the grade-school audience. It describes a few young friends one afternoon while they are playing, uneasily exchanging confidences about experiences with sexual abuse. As they talk among themselves, animated vignettes depict the problems in an explicit but not alarming way. The children consider possible solutions to their problems and agree to speak up and seek help from trusted adults. The film provides information about inappropriate touching and ways in which children can help themselves or their friends to work through solutions to a sensitive problem. This film is available from the National Center for the Prevention and Treatment of Child Abuse and Neglect (see p. 88). Additional sources of video material are listed on page 69.

Many teachers and families use storytelling to help prevent sexual abuse. They make up situations and discuss them, encouraging questions. They also play "What if" games, in which children are told stories and asked what they would do if certain situations happened to them. For example, Sandra's older sister asked her what she would do if a neighbor gave her a ride home from school and showed her some pictures of himself without any clothes on. What if this happened? What would she do?

Volunteers and the many people who provide financial support to organizations that are concerned with child abuse help to prevent it from happening. For example, the National Committee for the Prevention of Child Abuse is composed of thousands of volunteers who work with community, state, national, and international groups to expand and distribute knowledge about the prevention of child abuse. They work to stop abuse before it happens.

Diane Lozita is typical of those workers. She was able to make a unique contribution by designing ads with compelling public appeal as contributions to the program of the San Francisco Child Abuse Council. Volunteers in hundreds of communities make a wide variety of contributions to help awaken the public to the problems of child abuse. About 90 percent of the population of the United States is aware that child abuse is one of the nation's most serious social and public health problems. A much smaller percentage are aware of the extent of the problem of child sexual abuse, even though the victims of such tragedies are becoming much more visible.

Psychologists such as Professor George Albee of the University of Vermont are especially concerned with the primary prevention of child sexual abuse. Just as many contagious diseases could not be eradicated by helping individual victims, the problem of child sexual abuse cannot be eliminated by helping individual families, important though that may be. Professor Albee points out the need to change the cultural definition of appropriate male behavior. Rather than blaming poorly functioning families, Professor Albee and many other experts feel the need for development of different attitudes as boys grow up. Then there would be a more even distribution of power between the sexes.

For many families, the role of the father has already changed. He is no longer the forbidding and formidable figure of authority whose every word was law to wife and children. Many people see families who share in discipline and the making of important decisions as more mature families. The father is still respected for his achievements, his loving care, and other contributions, but he no longer "owns" his wife and children.

Many colleges and other schools are offering courses in fatherhood. They explore new roles for fathers and new ways they can help their children grow up with more self-esteem. They come to understand that it is wrong to use unequal physical, financial, social, or emotional power at the expense of their children. Men who are comfortable about relating to women at the same level of maturity as themselves are unlikely to exploit children sexually. Professor Albee suggests, "If we are to prevent sexual problems, we must prevent sexism by finding effective ways to redistribute power."

As men take on more equal responsibility for the care of children and become more sensitive to their needs, they learn how to enjoy deeply affectionate relationships that have no sexual components. Professor David Finkelhor suggests that this is one of the most important steps toward transforming men from offenders against children to defenders of their well-being.

Although vast progress has been made in dealing with the problems of child sexual abuse, it is still one of the most concealed and distressing forms of child abuse. You can help relatives, friends, and neighbors develop greater awareness of the problem. You can enlist their support for local prevention programs. Programs of treatment will not develop in a community without public support. You can distribute free materials such as those available from CHILDHELP USA and the National Committee for the Prevention of Child Abuse. You can encourage groups to choose the subject of child sexual abuse as a study program and point out the availability of inexpensive materials like those listed in the free catalog from the National Committee for the Prevention of Child Abuse. Child abuse is a community problem that can be prevented only at the community level.

You may be able to join the network of concerned citizens of the National Committee for the Prevention of Child Abuse if there is a chapter in your area. Write to the national office at 332 South Michigan Avenue, Suite 1250, Chicago, IL 60604-4357, for information about the chapter nearest you. You may wish to help organize a chapter if there is none in your area.

You can help to prevent child abuse by supporting education for parents, programs for abused children and young adults, life skills training for children and young adults, neighborhood support and self-help groups such as Parents Anonymous, public information and education on the prevention of child abuse, programs for new parents, and community organization activities that reduce family stress.

The National Child Abuse Coalition advocates continuing federal focus on the problems of all kinds of child abuse. More information can be obtained directly from the National Child Abuse Coalition, 1125 15th Street, N.W., Suite 300, Washington, DC 20005.

These are just some of the ways to raise awareness of and to help prevent the sexual abuse of children.

ADDITIONAL MATERIAL TO EXPLORE

ESPECIALLY FOR PRESCHOOL AND ELEMENTARY GRADES

Beaudry, Jo, and Ketchum, Lynne. *Carla Goes to Court*. Human Sciences Press, 1983.

Kleven, Sandra L. *The Touching Problem*. A one-hour program for children in elementary schools. Bellingham, Wash.: Coalition for Child Advocacy.

Krause, Elaine. *Speak Up, Say No*. Filmstrip. Preschool to second grade. Oregon City, Oreg.: Krause House.

Sweet, Phyllis. *Something Happened to Me*. Mother Courage Press, 1981.

White, Lori, and Spencer, Steve. *Take Care with Yourself*. Take Care with Yourself, 915 Maxine Road, Flint, MI 48503.

Williams, Joy. *Once I Was a Little Bit Frightened*. Fargo, N.Dak.: Rape and Abuse Crisis Center of Fargo-Moorhead, 1980.

———. *Red Flag, Green Flag People*. Fargo, N.Dak.: Rape and Abuse Crisis Center of Fargo-Moorhead, 1980.

FOR UPPER ELEMENTARY GRADES, JUNIOR HIGH, AND SENIOR HIGH SCHOOL

Bauer, Marion Dane. *Foster Child*. Seabury Press, 1977.

Daughters and Sons United. *Children Helping Children*. Booklet. San Jose, Calif.: Institute of the Community as Extended Family, 1981.

Faye, Jennifer J., and Flerchinger, Billy Jo. *Top Secret: Sexual Assault Information for Teenagers Only.* Booklet. Renton, Wash.: King County Rape Relief, no date.

Hyde, Margaret O. *Cry Softly! The Story of Child Abuse.* Westminster Press, 1980.

———. *My Friend Has Four Parents.* McGraw-Hill Book Co., 1981.

———. *My Friend Wants to Run Away.* McGraw-Hill Book Co., 1979.

Keating, Kathleen. *The Hug Therapy Book.* CompCare Publications, 1983.

Kyte, Kathy. *In Charge: A Complete Handbook for Kids with Working Parents.* Alfred A. Knopf, 1983.

———. *Play It Safe: The Kids' Guide to Personal Safety and Crime Prevention.* Alfred A. Knopf, 1983.

Contact the National Center for the Prevention and Treatment of Child Abuse and Neglect, 1205 Oneida Street, Denver, CO 80220, for information about additional materials. Some audiovisuals are available for rent from the center. Write for a complete annotated list of over one hundred items.

CHILD SEXUAL ABUSE TREATMENT CENTERS

The following list includes programs that were developed exclusively to treat child sexual abuse or that incorporate special components and resources to deal with some aspect of this problem. Also check in the Blue Pages of your local telephone directory.

Alaska

South Peninsula Women's
  Services
Box 2328
Homer, AL 99603

Women in Safe Homes
P.O. Box 6552
Ketchikan, AL 99901

Rape Incest Program
Judith Group, Inc.
P.O. Box 2334
Soldotna, AL 99669

Arizona

Behavior Associates
330 East 13th Street
Tucson, AZ 85701

Arkansas

SCAN (Suspected Child
  Abuse/Neglect)
University of Arkansas School
  of Social Work
33d and University
Little Rock, AR 72204

California

Incest Help, Inc.
719 Jackson Street
Albany, CA 94706

Families in Crisis Program
Psychological Associates
735 Duarte Road
Arcadia, CA 91006

Child Sexual Abuse
  Treatment Program
Solano County Department
  of Mental Health
1408 Pennsylvania Avenue
Fairfield, CA 94533

Family Crisis Center
Fresno County Department
  of Social Services
4455 East Wings Canyon
Fresno, CA 93750

Incest Awareness Project
Women's Resource Program
1213 North Highland
Hollywood, CA 90038

Lompoc Mental Health
  Services
Santa Barbara County Mental
  Health Services
401 East Cypress
Lompoc, CA 93436

Child Sexual Abuse Project
Los Angeles County
  Department of Social
  Services
5427 Whittier Boulevard
Los Angeles, CA 90022

Child Sexual Abuse
  Treatment Program
Child Protective Services
401 Broadway
Oakland, CA 74607

Riverside Inter-Agency
  Sexual Abuse Council
Riverside County
  Department of Public
  Social Services
4260 Tequesquite Avenue
Riverside, CA 92501

Child Sexual Abuse Program
Family Service Agency
1669 East Northeast Street
San Bernardino, CA 92405

Child Sexual Abuse
  Treatment Program
San Diego County
  Department of Welfare
6950 Levant Street
San Diego, CA 92111

Child and Adolescent Sexual
  Abuse Resource Center
San Francisco General
  Hospital Medical Center
1001 Potrero Avenue
San Francisco, CA 94110

Santa Clara County Child
  Abuse Program
840 Guadalupe Parkway
San Jose, CA 95011

Child Sexual Abuse
  Treatment Program
Marin County Department of
  Health and Human
  Services
P.O. Box 4160 Civic Center
  Branch
San Rafael, CA 94903

Child Abuse Sexual
   Treatment Program
Family Resource Center
500 Hilby
Seaside, CA 93955

Sexual Abuse Treatment
   Program
Forensic Psychology
   Associates
5430 Van Nuys Boulevard
Van Nuys, CA 91401

Colorado

Sexual Abuse Program
Boulder County Department
   of Social Services
3400 Broadway
Boulder, CO 80306

Child Protective Services
El Paso County Department
   of Social Services
P.O. Box 2692
105 North Spruce
Colorado Springs, CO 80901

Child Sexual Abuse
   Treatment Program
University of Colorado
   Medical Center
4200 East 9th Avenue
Denver, CO 80262

National Center for the
   Prevention and Treatment
   of Child Abuse and Neglect
1205 Oneida Street
Denver, CO 80220

Connecticut

Sex Crimes Unit
Connecticut State Police
   Department
Meriden, CT 06540

Sex Offender Program
Connecticut State
   Department of Corrections
P.O. Box 100
Somers, CT 06701

Waterbury Child Sexual
   Abuse Treatment Program
Waterbury Collaboration for
   the Prevention of Child
   Abuse and Neglect
56 Franklin Street
Waterbury, CT 06702

District of Columbia

Child Sexual Victim
   Assistance Project
Child Protection Center
Children's Hospital
   National Medical Center
111 Michigan Avenue
Washington, DC 20010

Sexual Abuse Prevention
   Program
D.C. Rape Crisis Center
P.O. Box 21005
Washington, DC 20009

Florida

Advocates for Sexually
Abused Children
Advocates for Victims
1515 N.W. 7th Street
Miami, FL 33125

Family Crisis Clinic
Jackson Memorial Hospital
1611 N.W. 12th Avenue
Miami, FL 33136

Victim-Court Liaison Services
State Attorney
9th Judicial Circuit
P.O. Box 1673
Orlando, FL 32801

Child Development Center
Community Mental Health
Center of Escambia
County
1201 West Hernandez
Pensacola, FL 32501

Child Protection Team
Suite 212
301 Broadway
Riviera Beach, FL 33404

Juvenile Welfare Board of
Pinellas County
4140 49th Street
St. Petersburg, FL 33709

Child Sexual Abuse
Treatment Program
Tampa Women's Health
Center, Inc.
3004 Fletcher
Tampa, FL 33612

Georgia

Rape Crisis Center
Grady Memorial Hospital
80 Butler Street
Atlanta, GA 30303

Hawaii

Child Sexual Abuse
Treatment Program
Catholic Social Service
250 South Vineyard Street
Honolulu, HI 96813

Parents United, Daughters
and Sons United
1060 Bethel Street
Honolulu, HI 96813

Sexual Abuse Treatment
Program
Kapiolani Children's Hospital
1319 Punahou Street
Honolulu, HI 96826

Idaho

Women's Crisis Center
Young Women's Christian
  Association
720 West Washington Street
Boise, ID 83702

Incest Program
Idaho State Department of
  Health and Welfare
431 Memorial Drive
Pocatello, ID 83201

Illinois

Child Sexual Abuse
  Treatment and Training
  Center
345 Manor Court
Bolingbrook, IL 60439

Child Abuse Unit for Studies,
  Education and Services
836 West Wellington Avenue
Chicago, IL 60657

Rape and Sexual Abuse Care
  Center
SIUE Box 154
Edwardsville, IL 62026

Council on Children at Risk
1630 Fifth Avenue
Moline, IL 61265

Indiana

Youth Services Bureau
Samuel Strong Building
330 West Lexington Street
Elkhart, IN 46514

Child Sexual Abuse
  Component
Marion County Department
  of Public Welfare
143 South Meridian Street
Indianapolis, IN 46225

Iowa

Domestic Violence Program
Catholic Social Services
Council Bluffs, IA 51501

Department of
  Pediatrics/Adolescent
  Clinic
University Hospital
Iowa City, IA 52242

Counseling for Sexual Abuse
Catholic Charities Diocese of
  Sioux City
Sioux City, IA 51104

Maine

Sexual Exploitation Project
Department of Mental
  Health and Corrections
Room 411
State Office Building
Augusta, ME 04333

Sexual Abuse Treatment
Program
Community Counseling
Center
622 Congress Street
Portland, ME 04101

Sexual Exploitation Project
Fairharbor Shelter
YWCA
Portland, ME 04101

Maryland

Multidisciplinary Committee
on Physical and Sexual
Abuse and Neglect
Anne Arundel County
Department of Social
Services
Arundel Center
44 Calvert Street
Annapolis, MD 21401

Sex Offense Task Force
Baltimore City State's
Attorney's Office
Criminal Courts Building,
Room 221
Baltimore, MD 21202

Sexual Abuse Treatment
Program
312 East Oliver Street
Baltimore City Department
of Social Services
Baltimore, MD 21202

Sexual Assault People
Program
Baltimore City Hospitals
Department of Medical
Social Work
4940 Eastern Avenue
Baltimore, MD 21224

Prince Georges Hospital
Sexual Assault Center
Prince Georges General
Hospital and Medical
Center
Hospital Drive
Cheverly, MD 20785

Family Assessment and
Treatment Program: Child
Sexual Abuse
Montgomery County
Department of Social
Services
5630 Fishers Lane
Rockville, MD 20852

National Center for the
Prevention and Control of
Rape
National Institute of Mental
Health
5600 Fishers Lane
Rockville, MD 20852

Sexual Abuse Treatment
Program
Protective Services Unit
Baltimore County
Department of Social
Services
620 York Road
Towson, MD 21204

76

Massachusetts

Sexual Abuse Treatment
Team
Children's Hospital Medical
Center
300 Longwood Avenue
Boston, MA 02115

Victim Counseling Service
Boston City Hospital
Department of Nursing
Services
818 Harrison Avenue
Boston, MA 02118

Center for Diagnosis and
Treatment of Sexually
Dangerous Persons
Massachusetts Department of
Mental Health
Bridgewater, MA 02324

Protective Services Unit
Massachusetts Department of
Welfare
75 Commercial Street
Brockton, MA 02402

Victims Support Group
260 River Drive
Hadley, MA 01035

Incest Consultation Network
P.O. Box 625
Northampton, MA 01060

Somerville Women's Mental
Health Collective
61 Roseland
Somerville, MA 02143

Incest Treatment Project
Baystate Medical Center
759 Chestnut Street
Springfield, MA 01107

Michigan

Victims Support Group
P.O. Box 7883
Ann Arbor, MI 48107

Bay City Office
Lutheran Child and Family
Service
P.O. Box B
Bay City, MI 48707

Special Family Problem
Services
Children's Aid Society of
Detroit
7700 2d Street
Detroit, MI 48202

Genesee County Child Abuse
Consortium
6th Avenue and Begole
Flint, MI 48502

Minnesota

Dakota Sexual Assault
Services
Community Action Council,
Inc.
13760 Nicollet Avenue South
Burnsville, MN 55337

Child Sexual Abuse
Prevention Program
Illusion Theatre and School
528 Hennepin Avenue, Room
309
Minneapolis, MN 55403

Christophe Street, Inc.,
Incest Program
2344 Nicollet Avenue South
Minneapolis, MN 55405

Judson Family Center
4101 Harriet Avenue South
Minneapolis, MN 55409

Sexual Assault Services
Hennepin County Attorney's
Office
C-2000 Government Center
Minneapolis, MN 55487

Center for Parents and
Children
1015 7th Avenue
Moorhead, MN 56560

Family Incest Program
Wilder Child Guidance Clinic
919 LaFond Road
St. Paul, MN 55104

Family Sexual Abuse
Treatment and Training
Program
Meta Recourses
821 Raymond Avenue
St. Paul, MN 55114

Ramsey County Community
Human Services
529 Jackson Street
St. Paul, MN 55101

Interagency Identification,
Intervention, and
Treatment of Incest
Winona County Department
of Social Services
157 Lafayette Street
Winona, MN 55987

Missouri

Child Sexual Abuse
Management Program
St. Louis Children's Hospital
500 South Kingshighway
Boulevard
P.O. Box 14871
St. Louis, MO 63178

Child Sexual Abuse
Treatment Program
Christian Family Life Center
6636 Clayton Road
St. Louis, MO 63117

Nebraska

Cat and Mouse
Girls Club of Omaha
3706 Lake Street
Omaha, NE 68111

Parents United and
Daughters and Sons United
of Sarpy and Douglas
Counties
1210 Golden Gate Drive
Papillon, NE 68046

New Jersey

Atlantic County Adolescent
Maltreatment Program
Division of Youth and Family
Services
26 South Pennsylvania
Avenue
Atlantic City, NJ 08401

Adult Diagnostic and
Treatment Center
Rahway Prison (Offenders
Program)
P.O. Box 190
Avenel, NJ 07001

Family Service of Burlington
County
Meadow Health Center
Woodlane Road
Mount Holly, NJ 08060

Incest Counseling Unit
New Jersey State Division of
Youth and Family Services
Mercer County District
Office
1901 North Olden Avenue
Trenton, NJ 08618

New York

Otsego County Council on
Child Abuse and Neglect
Bassett Hospital
P.O. Box 731
Cooperstown, NY 13326

Queensboro Society for the
Prevention of Cruelty to
Children
161–20 89th Avenue
Jamaica, NY 11432

New York Society for the
Prevention of Cruelty to
Children
110 East 71st Street
New York, NY 10021

Sex Crimes Prosecution Unit
New York County Office of
the District Attorney
155 Leonard Street
New York, NY 10013

Therapeutic Alternatives to
Sexual Abuse
Family Services of Rochester
30 North Clinton Avenue
Rochester, NY 14606

Alliance Child Abuse
Coordination Program
Catholic Charities
Family Services Division
1654 West Onondaga Street
Syracuse, NY 13204

79

Victims of Incest
Westchester Jewish
    Community Services
172 South Broadway
White Plains, NY 10605

North Carolina

Sexual Abuse Prevention
    Project
Alamance-Caswell Area
    Mental Health–Mental
    Retardation Program
407 South Broad Street
Burlington, NC 27215

North Carolina Sexual Abuse
    Identification and
    Treatment Project
Department of Social
    Services
325 North Salisbury Street
Raleigh, NC 27611

North Dakota

Sexual Assault Program
Rape and Abuse Crisis
    Center
Fargo, ND 58107

Rape Crisis Center
Grand Forks County Social
    Service Center
118 North 3d Street
Grand Forks, ND 58201

Jamestown Area Sexual
    Abuse Treatment Unit
Jamestown Area Social
    Services Center
Box 334
Jamestown, ND 58401

Ohio

Cleveland Rape Crisis Center
3201 Euclid Avenue
Cleveland, OH 44115

Sexual Abuse
    Treatment/Training
    Project
Federation for Community
    Planning
1001 Huron Road
Cleveland, OH 44115

Child Assault Prevention
    Program
Women Against Rape
P.O. Box 02084
Columbus, OH 43202

Child Sexual Abuse Program
Child and Family Services
535 Marmion Avenue
Youngstown, OH 44504

Oklahoma

Pediatric Psychology Service
Oklahoma Children's
  Memorial Hospital
Box 26901
900 N.E. 13th Street
Oklahoma City, OK 73104

Public Health Guidance
  Center
Oklahoma State Department
  of Health
N.E. 10th and Stonewall
  Streets
Oklahoma City, OK 73105

At-Risk-Parent-Child
  Program
Hillcrest Medical Center and
  the University of Oklahoma
College of Medicine
Utica on the Park
Tulsa, OK 74104

Oregon

Adolescent Victims
  Counseling Groups
Oregon Department of
  Human Resources
Children's Service Division
1102 Lincoln Street
Eugene, OR 97401

Christian Family Institute
Counseling Services
1501 Pearl Street
Eugene, OR 97401

Incest Treatment Program
1188 S.W. 4th Street
Ontario, OR 97914

Child Abuse Sexual
  Treatment Program
Child Protective Services
1031 East Burnside
Portland, OR 97215

Child Incest Treatment
  Program
Parents United, Inc.
3905 S.E. Belmont, Suite 1
Portland, OR 97214

Mid-Valley Center Against
  Domestic and Sexual
  Violence
P.O. Box 851
Salem, OR 97308

Pennsylvania

Incest Counseling Program
  and INNOCENSE (Rap
  Group for Women Victims)
Women Organized Against
  Rape in Bucks County
P.O. Box 793
Langhorne, PA 19047

Incest and Sexual Abuse
  Program
Joseph J. Peters Institute
112 South 16th Street
Philadelphia, PA 19102

81

Sexual Abuse Advocacy
Program
Women Organized Against
Rape
1220 Sansom Street
Philadelphia, PA 19107

Parents United
Parents Anonymous of
Pittsburgh
1718 Allegheny Building
429 Forbes Avenue
Pittsburgh, PA 15219

Tennessee

Project Against Sexual Abuse
of Appalachian Children
Child and Family Services of
Knox County, Inc.
114 Dameron Avenue
Knoxville, TN 37917

Sex Abuse Help Line
Child and Family Services of
Knox County, Inc.
114 Dameron Avenue
Knoxville, TN 37917

Child Sex Abuse Technical
Assistance Project
Tennessee Department of
Human Services
Social Service Department
410 State Office Building
Nashville, TN 37219

Texas

Dallas Sexual Abuse Project
Texas Department of Human
Resources
Social Services Branch
John H. Reagan Building
Austin, TX 78701

Sex Abuse Counseling
Program
Family Service Association
230 Pereida Street
San Antonio, TX 78210

Virginia

Parents United—
Fredericksburg Chapter
Fifteenth District Court
Service Unit
601 Caroline Street
Fredericksburg, VA 22401

Norfolk Family Sexual
Trauma Team
Norfolk Police Department
P.O. Box 358
Norfolk, VA 23501

North West Center for
Community Mental Health
11420 Isaac Newton Square
Reston, VA 22090

Sexual Abuse Treatment
Program
Virginia Department of
Social Services Municipal
Center
Virginia Beach, VA 23456

Washington

Lewis County Hotline
P.O. Box 337
Chehalis, WA 98532

Incest Treatment Program
Family Services of Kind
County
31003 18th Avenue South
Federal Way, WA 98003

Domestic Violence Program
Washington State
Department of Social and
Health Services
Olympia, WA 98504

Victims of Sexual Assault
Washington State
Department of Social and
Health Services
Olympia, WA 98504

Committee for Children
Seattle Institute for Child
Advocacy
P.O. Box 15190
Seattle, WA 98405

Juvenile Sex Offender
Treatment Program
Adolescent Clinic
University of Washington
Seattle, WA 98195

Sexual Assault Center
Harborview Medical Center
Seattle, WA 98104

Teenage Abuse Prevention
Program
Center for the Prevention of
Sexual and Domestic
Violence
4250 South Mead
Seattle, WA 98118

Rape Crisis Network
Lutheran Social Services of
Washington
Spokane, WA 99201

Child Sexual Abuse and
Treatment Program
Tacoma School District
P.O. Box 1357
Tacoma, WA 98401

Incest: Community
Treatment Model in
Children's Protective
Services
Washington State County
Community Services
420 East 115th Street
Tacoma, WA 98402

Incest Family Services
P.O. Box 44608
Tacoma, WA 98444

Pierce County Rape Relief
Allenmore Medical Center
South 19th and Union
	Avenue
Tacoma, WA 98405

Sexual Assault Program
Central Washington
	Comprehensive Mental
	Health
Yakima, WA 98901

West Virginia

Sexual Abuse Treatment and
	Training
3375 Route 60 East
P.O. Box 8069
Huntington, WV 25705

Wisconsin

Parental Stress Center, Inc.
1506 Madison Street
Madison, WI 53711

Rape Crisis Center
312 East Wilson Street
Madison, WI 53703

Incest Treatment Service
Family Hospital
2711 West Wells Street
Milwaukee, WI 53208

Parents Anonymous,
	Intrafamily Sexual Abuse
	Program
Parents Anonymous of
	Greater Milwaukee
P.O. Box 11415
Milwaukee, WI 53211

SOURCES OF
FURTHER INFORMATION

Bubblyonian Productions, Inc.
  7204 West 80th Street, Overland Park, KS 66204

CHILDHELP USA
National Campaign for the Prevention of Child Abuse and
  Neglect
National Headquarters, Woodland Hills, CA 91370

Coalition for Child Advocacy
  P.O. Box 159, Bellingham, WA 98227

Daughters and Sons United
  P.O. Box 952, San Jose, CA 95108-0952

Illusion Theatre Company
  528 Hennepin Ave., Rm. 309, Minneapolis, MN 55403

Institute of the Community as Extended Family
  P.O. Box 952, San Jose, CA 95108-0952

King County Rape Relief
  305 South 43d Street, Renton, WA 98055

Maltreatment of Youth Project
  Boys Town Center for Study of Youth Development
  Boys Town, NE 68010

National Center for the Prevention and Treatment of Child
   Abuse and Neglect
   1205 Oneida Street, Denver, CO 80220

National Center on Child Abuse and Neglect
Children's Bureau
Administration for Children, Youth, and Families
   U.S. Department of Health and Human Services
   P.O. Box 1182, Washington, DC 20013

National Child Abuse Coalition
   1125 15th Street, N.W., Suite 300, Washington, DC 20005

National Committee for the Prevention of Child Abuse
   332 South Michigan Avenue, Suite 1250
   Chicago, IL 60604-4357

Parents Anonymous
   22330 Hawthorne Boulevard, Suite 208
   Torrance, CA 90505

Parents United
   P.O. Box 952, San Jose, CA 95108-0952

San Francisco Child Abuse Council, Inc.
   4093 24th Street, San Francisco, CA 94114

Sexual Assault Services
Office of the Hennepin County Attorney
   2000-C Government Center, Minneapolis, MN 55487

Many community resources for volunteer opportunities or
help can be located through the United Way in your community
and through your telephone book. Look under Comprehensive
Community Services, United Way Community Services, or Information Line in the White Pages, or Social Services in the
Yellow Pages. Or contact United Way, Services Outreach Division, 801 North Fairfax Street, Alexandria, VA 22314.

REGIONAL CHILD ABUSE AND NEGLECT RESOURCE CENTERS

The centers listed below are funded by the U.S. Department of Health and Human Services. Each center has a child abuse and neglect component, and each provides a wide range of information, including programs, materials, services, and possible volunteer opportunities in the community. Contact the center that serves your state.

Region I (serving Connecticut, Maine, Massachusetts, New Hampshire, Rhode Island, Vermont): Resource Center for Children and Families, Judge Baker Guidance Center, 295 Longwood Avenue, Boston, MA 02115.

Region II (serving New Jersey, New York, Puerto Rico, Virgin Islands): Resource Center for Children and Youth Services, Cornell University, Family Life Development Center, College of Human Ecology, E 200 MVR, Ithaca, NY 14853.

Region III (serving Delaware, District of Columbia, Maryland, Pennsylvania, Virginia, West Virginia): Resource Center for Children, Youth, and Families, Virginia Commonwealth University, School of Social Work, 1001 W. Franklin Street, Richmond, VA 23284.

Region IV (serving Alabama, Florida, Georgia, Kentucky, Mississippi, North Carolina, South Carolina, Tennessee): Resource Center for Children and Youth Services, University of Tennessee, School of Social Work, 1838 Terrace Avenue, Knoxville, TN 37996.

Region V (serving Illinois, Indiana, Michigan, Minnesota, Ohio, Wisconsin): Resource Center on Children and Youth Services, University of Wisconsin at Milwaukee, School of Social Welfare, P.O. Box 786, Milwaukee, WI 53201.

Region VI (serving Arkansas, Louisiana, New Mexico, Oklahoma, Texas): Resource Center for Children, Youth, and Families, University of Texas at Austin, 2609 University Avenue, Austin, TX 78712.

Region VII (serving Iowa, Kansas, Missouri, Nebraska): Children, Youth, and Family Resource Center, University of Iowa—Oakdale Campus, Institute of Child Behavior and Development, Oakdale, IA 52319.

Region VIII (serving Colorado, Montana, North Dakota, South Dakota, Utah, Wyoming): Family Resource Center, University of Denver, Graduate School of Social Work, Denver, CO 80208.

Region IX (serving Arizona, California, Guam, Hawaii, Nevada, Pacific Trust Territories): Resource Center for Children, Youth, and Families, California State University at Los Angeles, 5151 State University Drive, Los Angeles, CA 90032.

Region X (serving Alaska, Idaho, Oregon, Washington): Northwest Resource Center for Children, Youth, and Families, University of Washington, School of Social Work, 4101 15th Avenue, N.E., Seattle, WA 98195.

I N D E X

ABOUT THE AUTHOR

MARGARET O. HYDE is author of an outstanding list of books for young people including *My Friend Wants to Run Away; Addictions: Gambling, Smoking, Cocaine Use, and Others; Fears and Phobias; Know About Smoking; Crime and Justice in Our Time;* and *Suicide: The Hidden Epidemic,* with Elizabeth Held Forsyth. Mrs. Hyde has written documentaries for NBC-TV and taught children, young adults, and adults.